An Extravagant Way of Saying Nothing

And as I consider
how this could be an analogy
on my life as a child of God,
my cats are in the corner,
wondering ...
when I'll refill the water bowl.

~ James Roethlein

Also by James Roethlein

Musing on the Cricket Game of Life – Part 1 ½

An Extravagant Way of Saying Nothing

James Roethlein

720 Sixth Street, Unit #5
New Westminster, BC
V3L 3C5
CANADA

Title: An Extravagant Way of Saying Nothing
Author: James Roethlein
Publisher: Silver Bow Publishing
Cover Layout and Design: Candice James
Editing: Candice James

All rights reserved including the right to reproduce or translate this book or any portions thereof, in any form without the permission of the publisher. Except for the use of short passages for review purposes, no part of this book may be reproduced, in part or in whole, or transmitted in any form or by any means, either by means electronically or mechanically, including photocopying, recording, or any information or storage retrieval system without prior permission in writing from the publisher or a licence from the Canadian Copyright Collective Agency (Access Copyright).

www.silverbowpublishing.com
info@silverbowpublishing.com
ISBN: 978-1-77403-118-6 paperback
ISBN: 978-1-77403-119-3 electronic book
© Silver Bow Publishing

Library and Archives Canada Cataloguing in Publication

Title: An extravagant way of saying nothing / James Roethlein.
Names: Roethlein, James, 1971- author.
Description: Poems.
Identifiers: Canadiana (print) 20200271571 | Canadiana (ebook) 20200272403 | ISBN 9781774031186
 (softcover) | ISBN 9781774031193 (EPUB)
Classification: LCC PS3618.O38 E98 2020 | DDC 811/.6—dc23

An Extravagant Way of Saying Nothing

for Mr. Hollich
who helped start me on this path.

and

In memory of Holly Warden,
never completely forgotten

An Extravagant Way of Saying Nothing

Table of Contents

Must I Always ... 9
Mansion of Memories ... 10
Another Dark Poem ... 11
Sometimes the Muse of My Poetry, is Poetry ... 12
Days to Remember ... 13
Down One Third ... 14
Ocean Mist Whispers ... 15
An ... 16
It's the Friday ... 17
Ponder the Pursuit ... 18
You'll Never See Me Coming ... 19
Where Satan Stands ... 20
Waters of Winter ... 21
Horse-blinded ... 22
Solace in Stillness ... 23
And a Trumpet Shall Call Them ... 24
Fun in the Fog ... 25
Observer of Life ... 26
Night Visitors ... 27
The Honey Sweet Stomach Turning Scroll ... 28
Ten Thousand Pyres ... 29
Untitled ... 30
Death Was Arrested ... 31
Ebony Fair ... 32
The Mornings as Midnight ... 33
Lady Godiva (with her clothes on) ... 34
Love in Whispers .. 35
Modern Day Lady of La Mancha ... 36
Hope of a Story ... 37
Post Modern Love Affair ... 38
End of Date ... 39
When Will, Then Will ... 40
He Wishes She'd Leave the Lights On ... 41
Kiss and Tell ... 42
You Are the Morning 43
Valley of Decision ... 44
Honey Sweet ... 45
They Each Dreamed ... 46
I Remember You ... 47
Angered Silence ... 48

He Waited to Watch ... 49
Winter Fall Winter ... 50
Dream Faces ... 51
Deified 'Membrances ... 52
Chasm's Edge ... 53
Shadow Bound ... 54
A World of Hurt ... 55
Thirty Souls Standing ... 56
The Flight of Gulls ... 57
The Poem Has Decided ... 58
Affection Flows ... 59
Cracks and Fissures ... 60
At the Lord's Table ... 61
Kaleidoscope of Sound ... 62
Leg Zeppelin ... 63
A Fool's Wish ... 64
A Final Gasp Before Oblivion ... 65
More to This Life ... 66
Tears as Winter Rain ... 67
The Poem ... 68
Daily I Clean My Cup ... 69
Soul Self Staring ... 70
Unsettled Soul ... 71
The Breakdown ...72
Early Morning Waking Dream ...73
The Dead Room ... 74
Days as Minutes ... 75
Happy Me, Sad Me, Real Me ... 76
A Taste of Freedom ... 77
Angels on the Edge of Heaven ... 78
On the Praises Rising ... 79
Three in Heaven ... 80
Battle Remembrances ... 81
Victory ... 82
Ares' Aim ... 83
The World as a Cookie ... 84
Imaginative, Idle Mind ... 85
Bare Knuckle Boxing Against Brick Walls ... 86
Love ... 87

Must I Always

Poems from pain
with its muse of a heart broken
before it learns to love,
for in a world
of joy's fountains overflowing,
my wellspring is sorrow.

But must I always write from there?

Mansion of Memories

These four walls,
no longer mine.
The mansion of my memories
is letting me go,
that it may adopt a new family.

As the chapter wanes,
the page turns to a new season,
and a new home
that will call me its own.

Another Dark Poem

Another dark poem
of a terminal future,
bodies decaying,
scattered without graves,
for the dead
never bury their own.

Sometimes the Muse of My Poetry is Poetry

Sometimes the muse of my poetry is poetry
speaking through the fact of it being,
if not through what the poet wrote.

And it comes to me at all hours,
insistent, unrelenting
as a cat's or baby's cry
that will not be ignored.

Days to Remember

Days to remember
upon the river of time,
age to determine
a slow or quick passing
to the place appointed,
where eternity begins.

Down One Third

Down one third,
Son God; dead.
Three days hence,
Son God; rose.
Man soul, free
of knife's edge.

Ocean Mist Whispers

Ocean mist whispers
as crashing waves,
speaking to me shore-side
of this time-bound earth,
then ask,
do I love Him more than these?

An

An, I remember.
An, I can't forget.
Anne, I sometimes wonder
where you are now.

It's the Friday

It's the Friday movies are named for.
But hockey-masked murderers,
the least of my worries,
with mirrors, ladders, and sidewalk cracks,
working for the cats in black,
are out to get me because they can,
and want to.

Ponder the Pursuit

Pondering the pursuit
of a poorly penned poem,
proving,
I'm not always #1 with a bullet.

And as I consider
how this could be an analogy
on my life as a child of God,
my cats are in the corner,
wondering ...
when I'll refill the water bowl.

You'll Never See Me Coming

You'll never see me coming
and, because you aren't looking,
you'll never see me leave.

Where Satan Stands

A life-long's longing to be
standing where you are,
and I am there
knee deep in the water
where the riptide flows.

Say goodbye to the morning.
Wave farewell to the night,
and stand where Satan stands,
willing to face the music,
never knowing the tune.

Waters of Winter

Waters of winter
descending as they should,
cover the inventions of man
in ev'ry manner nature intends.

Horse-blindered

Horse-blindered eyes,
seeing nothing beyond
his droplet
in the vast ocean
of life and its concerns.

Reward determined
at the dust to dust destiny,
the whirligig of time
and the world's revenges
having their say.

Solace in Stillness

Solace in stillness,
silence the salve
soothing this self-seared soul.

Sending you away,
shutting the door behind,
I face loneliness alone
to let it die.

And a Trumpet Shall Call Them

And a trumpet shall call them,
shattering silence and the night.
Water to cleanse, holy fire to temper,
a motley crew let loose upon the world
(emboldened by lamb's blood and the rising),
turning its bottom rail on its many thrones.

Fun in the Fog

Outside with a knife
to cut at the rolling dark
beneath the muted glow of streetlights,
for no other logical reason
than to say I've done it.

Observer of Life

Observer of life
watching the world from his window
overlooking two city streets,
takes notes on life being lived,
but will not come down
and live it himself.

Night Visitors

Invading the store
(sometime before the witching hour),
thieves for money
(the love of it in their hearts).

Weapons drawn,
my mind turned blank.

God in His purpose
intended eternity to claim me
another day.

The Honey-Sweet Stomach-Turning Scroll
Rev. 10:9-11

Words honey sweet,
sour in the stomach
of those who carry
the message of future things
for any ears among the nations,
willing to listen,
willing to repent.

Ten Thousand Pyres

Ten thousand pyres
burning for the fallen.
Ten million more
coming to join them.

'Cause men with their history
of folly, fear, and pride,
will always be s ow to give up
the love of waging war.

Untitled
(in memory of Lewis K. Webster)

Another piece
of the puzzle,
of the present
passing to the past,
waiting in eternity
for us to return home.

Death was Arrested

Death
was arrested.
Death
was tried.
Death
was convicted.

When my Savior died.
When my Savior rose.

Death
will die.
Death
will die.

Death
will be put to death
when my Savior returns in glory.

Ebony Fair

Ebony fair
and lovely, a woman
dwelling in my dreams,
soapstone eyes, soft
to soften diamond hearts
and settle the soul.

But in the light of day,
caught in the gaze
of reality's stare,
I fear what I feel
lacks substance
beyond the hours
in which I slumber,
and dream of you.

The Mornings as Midnight

The mornings as midnight,
evenings under moonless skies,
a heart trapped in arctic winter
waiting in the frozen air of longing
for spring to finally come
in another woman's sunshine smile.

Lady Godiva (with her clothes on)

Lady Godiva (with her clothes on),
a modern goddess (in poetic terms)
is living next door.

Pleasant words exchanged in passing,
and a hint of longing lingers,
tickling at my soul.

I simply must ask her,

Love in Whispers

Love in whispers,
silent to me,
though she is there
on the other side of this wall.

Longing's lament takes shape
and leaves, no longer welcome.

Modern Day Lady of La Mancha

She is aware.
She does not care
I've made her my lady,
so long as I continue
to fight windmills
elsewhere.

Hope of a Story

An offer
of an unlocked door
in the hope
of a story written in tandem.
One that ends
where eternity begins.

Post-Modern Love Affair

Heart to heart,
hammer and chisel
molding it to my liking.

It will turn to dust
when my interest wanes.

End of Date

A tender kiss,
lightly on the lips,
fingertips and foreheads touching,
their eyes closed, fearful to open
lest they find the other disappeared.

And under the porchlight,
they linger together,
wishing this moment
would never end.

When Will, Then Will

When will
I look into your open eyes
at the break of ev'ry day?

Then will
I know you love me,
'cause you've chosen to stay.

He Wishes She'd Leave the Lights On

Streetlamps outside glowing,
silhouette her form
as she slips in on top,
and he wishes,
she'd leave the lights on.

Kiss and Tell

A secret spoken
ceases to be,
and the ways of my lover
in our bedroom,
something I'll never tell
when I find out.

You Are the Morning

You are the morning to me,
and I will wait
'til you are the afternoon
and evening as well.

Valley of Decision

The dawn of day
of seven years' ending,
pitch as night,
obsidian as men's darkened souls.

Murders of crows
descending,
circling,
feasting upon
the armies of Earth,
fallen in their final rebel yell.

Honey Sweet

Her honey so very sweet,
but who will taste it
with what the age demands?

Her blessing of beauty, a curse,
and the ordinary, extolled
as a higher virtue.

They Each Dreamed

They each dreamed
of being in the other's arms.

For her, it was the nightmare
she did not want.

For him, it was the vision
he could not have.

I Remember You

I remember you:
the one who tock my hand,
leading me to a place
where love is never found,
and leaving me there.

Angered Silence

In angered silence
the inches become miles.

How many thousand
lie between us?

He Waited to Watch

He waited to watch her leave,
not for love's sake,
but the slow drifting
to this moment of no turning back,
and the final certainty,
of never seeing her again
as she disappeared from sight.

Winter Fall Winter

Heart led,
winter to fall
to winter once more,
leaving you
is leaving me, free
for endurance of winter's end
before a waiting spring.

Dream Faces

Dream faces
long since vanished,
nightmares and fantasies
never to return,
and in the longing
for both terror and tenderness,
melodic melancholy
is a balm.

Deified 'Membrances

Deified 'membrances,
pyramid masters
to pyramid slaves.

No moments of separation
possible or allowed,
for cat calls and cat stares
follow me ev'rywhere I go.

Even to my throne room.

Chasm's Edge

A view compelling me
to write what I see,
lest I come back,
with face paint and green hair
in a special kind of crazy.

Shadow Bound

Shadow bound
in quick manner
as I stepped out,
a door closed gently,
is still a door closed.

A World of Hurt

A world of hurt, springing
from the answer you gave.
The deluge of pain, raining emotion:
only in my head,
only in my head
only in my head.
only in my head
and nowhere else.

Thirty Souls Standing

Thirty souls standing.
A silent talking throng.

Nary a voice among them
for a deaf man to hear.

Deep in conversation's art,
perhaps they're telepathic.

Perhaps just on their phones.

The Flight of Gulls

He fears
the flight of gulls
under cold grey skies,
and dreads the storm
(they're fleeing from)
bringing bad omens
upon the ill wind
blowing in its wake.

The Poem Has Decided

The poem has decided
it is an English sonnet
instead of the four-line free verse
it actually is.

Affection Flows

My affection flows
as bottled wine.

Will you take s sip?
Will you drink me dry?

Cracks and Fissures

Cracks and fissures
of so fragile a thing.

If what rends the heart
is not love, then what is it?

At the Lord's Table

Wafers
and wine
to remember.

Redemption
at a cost:
the Body,
and the Blood.

Kaleidoscope of Sound

Lend an ear, and listen
to the kaleidoscope of sound.
The inexpressible expression
via spoken word and song.

Pay heed to the medley
of motley muses meshing
the separate parts of a greater whole,
offering through the audible
the unseen things we live for.

Leg Zeppelin

Leg like a zeppelin,
twice the size it should be.

Much like the ego,
over-inflated,
ever ready for the fall.

A Fool's Wish

I remember
the years forgotten,
longing
for a reversal of fortune,
and those years forgotten.

A Final Gasp Before Oblivion

The worlds of other men
lie beyond his notice,
caring for nothing
but his own.

His world is his oyster,
and in his wake,
ev'rything breathes
a final gasp before oblivion.

More to This Life

There is more to this life
than what we seek
pursuant to happiness
and a longing to be loved.

For there is a dove in the sky,
and a snake in the garden,
either of each unseen by fools
at the expense of the soul.

Tears as Winter Rain

Tears as winter rain,
freezing the fire
of your autumn anger,
and so you chocse,
to never cry again.

The Poem

The poem,
like the spice must flow,
flowing as a river
rapid to the sea.

And damn the poet
who gives us verse
moving like a tortoise
trying to cross the street.

Daily I Clean My Cup

Daily
I clean
my cup
on the
outside
only.

Soul Self-Staring

Soul self-staring
mirror side back,
evil eye accusers
from what you see.

But rather than change
the rebel you inside,
you celebrate your own
personal Dorian Gray.

Unsettled Soul

His unsettled soul,
suddenly so
and at mid-sentence,
suddenly saw
he had nothing eft
to...

The Breakdown

One-way mental boxing matches:
pain turns to tears,
intense, constant, unrelenting;
the psyche upon the rack;
and tears morphing to laughter,
hysterical, the mind trapped
in its personal iron maiden.

Early Morning Waking Dream

With the onslaught
of a waking dream,
the alarm went off
driving it away.

The Dead Room
"a room without books is like a body without a soul"
  ~ Cicero

The dead room
(devoid of books),
offers what
the living and bedroom
never could:
the means to live,
so I can have a reason to.

Days as Minutes

Days as minutes,
one thing done
while onto the next.

Living a frantic, panicked pace
of now not then,
and we die two days
before Death expects us.

Happy Me, Sad Me, Real Me

Happy me; gone.
Sad me; stays.

Where and what
is real me?

A Taste of Freedom

A taste of freedom,
open, offered,
and they come
across deserts,
over the seven seas.

Huddled masses,
passing through the gate
(as husbands, wives,
and children)
yearning to be free.

Angels on the Edge of Heaven

Angels on the edge of Heaven
watched, from eternity,
events unfold upon the temporal plane.

The child of promise (announced to shepherds)
grew to glory for the purposed death:
to save all mankind.

Oh the Praises Rising

Oh the praises rising,
angelic voices in exaltation.

Shepherds and Persian kings
seek Him out.

Moses and Elijah coming together
this blessed night,
as Joshua breathes His earthly first,
and cries a baby's cry.

Three in Heaven

Three in Heaven
reduced to two,
the Son as a human child,
then a man,
showing shades of glory
to shepherds, thieves,
and fishermen.

Battle Remembrances

Set stone and markers,
reason to stand and remember,
how a town hid from fire and thunder
when the king of spades arrived.

Three days of blood and bullets,
bugle call and cannon blast,
the snapping turtle compelled to come
and forced to bring a fight.

A last desperate charge,
then tired retreat.

The heavens opened up:
God weeping rain
for both the living and the dead.

Victory

Mourning the loss
it has taken us
to win the war.

And in the winning,
is the loss greater
than what we gain?

Ares' Aim

No one left.
No one left.
No one left.

And still we appease him.

The World as a Cookie

The world as a cookie,
crumbling, dried out
(having killed all poets),
trampled to dust,
it sleeps in oblivion.

Imaginative, Idle Mind

Imaginative mind
in idle mode,
plaything for devils' hands.

Word weapons
sharper than knives,
arm those of evil passions,
deep in demon schemes,
destining the world to oblivion.

Bare Knuckle Boxing Against Brick Walls

Rage, rage
with bloodied fists.

I rage,
the world showing burlap love
to my brillo pad affection.

And so it must burn.

Love

Life comes in crayons.
Love only uses red.

www.ingramcontent.com/pod-product-compliance
Lightning Source LLC
Chambersburg PA
CBHW062144100526
44589CB00014B/1683